SoulCry : book three

RESTORATION
FOR THE WOUNDED SOUL

an intimate poetic
expression of the deep
longings and cries of the soul

Have mercy on me, O God, according to your unfailing love.
Restore to me the joy of your salvation
And grant me a willing spirit
To sustain me.
Psalm 51:1,12 (NIV)

Trudy Colflesh

Bridal Cry

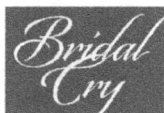

Bridalcry Publishing

Colorado Springs, CO

Cover and page design by Nathan Fisher, www.ideasablaze.com

ISBN 978-1-7320922-0-4

Additional Copies Available

Order at www.encouraginghope.com/soulcry

Table of Contents

DISSOCIATION

Foreword

The Lord desires that each of us as His children come to full maturity and wholeness so we can walk in the security of His love and come to the realization of our value and worth as an individual.

There is no perfect family and no perfect environment. Very few children, if any, escape childhood without being emotionally or physically damaged in some way, either intentionally or unintentionally.

Healthier families will provide the love and security needed to help the infant attach emotionally and develop a sense of being wanted and belonging. The child will begin to have an understanding of his or her identity as an individual and be accepted for him or herself. The child will feel heard. He or she will have confidence to learn and explore new skills without shame or criticism. Ideally, the child is lovingly guided through all the stages of childhood to maturity.

Sadly, even the best of environments will bring wounds. If the wounding is not noticed or addressed, the child will often create the belief that he or she is the reason and fault of the damage.

Because of the Grace and Mercy of God, it is not too late to be healed and restored from all the unhealed wounding and trauma of the past.

This book speaks the pain of the wounded soul, struggling to understand his or her feelings, often coming to wrong conclusions, wondering if anyone cares. Yet another voice, God's voice, speaks in *Restoration for the Wounded Soul* to bring hope and healing.

Let yourself hear the cry of your own soul as you read the poems. Allow the Lord to lovingly minister to your wounded soul. It's never too late to be healed.

ABOUT THE NOTEBOOK PAGES:

The Soul is expressing its deep cries
of emotion in the notebook pages.

About the Scroll:

The Lord responds to the cry of the Soul in the scrolls.

STOLEN IDENTITY

What do you mean
You wanted me to be you?

God didn't give me to you
So I could be cloned.

I came unique and
Wonderfully different,

Until you started,
With every word, every action, every look
To form and shape
Your likeness
Into me.

I needed love.
I didn't complain.
You seemed to know
What was best.

But I didn't know
My every thought,
My every feeling
Was quietly being conformed
Into your image.

The transformation complete,
I thought like you.
I acted like you.
I made you proud.

And you paraded me
For all to see
How wonderful you are
To have a child like me.

HER WONDERFUL DAUGHTER

I'm her wonderful daughter
But I think something's wrong.
Help me, Lord.

I don't know what I think,
But I know what she wants.

I don't know how I feel,
But I know how to make her happy.

I'm her wonderful daughter.
She tells me that all the time.
We're like two peas in a pod.
She's like me and I'm like her.

But I think something's wrong.
It feels like I'm living her life,
Supporting her success
By being successful.

Who am I anyway?
Am I her, is she me?
It seemed okay for awhile
But how can this be?

Sometimes I fail
And let her down.
It feels so shameful
To not be
Wonderful.

Yet unaware of who I am,
She rewards me with enthusiastic praise
And words of cheer.
Though not deserved,
It does help soothe the gnawing pain
I hide... from both of us...
That I'm really not that wonderful.

I don't want to hurt her
Or disappoint her expectations.
I want to do better,
But something's wrong.

Would it be okay, Jesus,
To just be ordinary,
Inadequate,
Not always wonderful
Me?

I HAVE TO DISAPPOINT YOU

I have to disappoint you.
I'm sorry.

I've tried as hard as I can
To be all you wanted me to be,
But I just can't do it anymore.

I can't live your dreams,
Make you look good,
Be your reason to be proud.

It just won't work anymore.
I'm quitting.

I'm disappointing you.
I'm breaking the rules.

I have failed.
I am truly sorry.

Here's your life back.
Maybe you can make it work.

REFLECTION

(this is a space for you to write your thoughts)

I CAN'T KEEP DOING THIS

I can't keep doing this.
Being brave,
Being strong,
Just holding it all in
And going on.

I just want to
Break down and weep.
It's too hard.
Can't you see?

I hurt so badly.
I feel so needy.
I can't pretend anymore.

I can't keep doing this.
I'm just too tired.
There's no strength left.

I QUIT!

REFLECTION

(this is a space for you to write your thoughts)

SWITCHED AT BIRTH

"You got switched at birth.
I formed you for myself,"
Says God,
"I created your DNA
For you to be uniquely you.

"But you got switched at birth.
Your true identity was hidden,
Concealed.
No "missing" signs were posted.

"The truth was kept
From even you.
For all you knew
You were someone else.

"But I knew differently.
As good as you looked,
You were not the child
To whom I gave life.

"You were overlaid with
False identity,
Pretending, behaving,
But not living
From your heart.

"Then one day
You looked my way.
Your eyes fixed on mine,
And saw the you
I formed.

"With joyful recognition
We embraced!
You stepped into
The you that has your face.

"Found at last
You were set free
To live and laugh
And truly be."

AUTHOR'S COMMENTS

It may be surprising to realize that extensive praise can be as damaging as shame and criticism. Both impact a child's identity. Praise is best if attached to a specific accomplishment, like "You did a great job cleaning your room." Too many words like, "You are great, wonderful, outstanding, perfect," can become damaging to a good self-image. A child knows she* can't measure up to such continual praise but attempts to please by trying to be perfect. She can shut down and not allow true praise to build her identity, throwing out even healthy praise as false and not deserved. The child learns to hide the imperfect part and ends up shaming her own projected "perfect self."

However, praise should not always be attached to works. Healthy praise speaks to the child's being. She is loved because she is lovable. She is special and uniquely wonderful and is God's gift to her family and the world.

Unhealthy praise teaches the child to be the person the parent wants her to be rather than allowing her to be a normally growing child who is not always nice or perfect. She is brought into a codependent relationship with the parent, where the praise becomes a programming for her to keep her parent happy by her behavior. In return, she creates a compliant self that gets accepted.

But God places in our spirit an unrest until we break free into the person He has always destined us to be, not living out the design of another. He calls us into our true identity.

*The comments throughout the book apply to both females and males, but the female adjective will be used for ease of reading.

THOUGHTS TO JOURNAL

• In what ways was I controlled as a child? How was praise used?

• Did I learn to assert my own identity in a negative or positive way?

• Am I still trying to keep my parents happy and not being authentic with them?

• Do I know how the Lord sees me?

PRAYER

Dear Lord, Please help me know who you created me to be. Help me break codependent relationships that only hide and confuse my true identity. I choose to forgive my parents and other adults who tried to form me into the image they wanted. You have created me in your image. Help me believe and accept the love, value and worth you place on me. Thank you that you can heal my sense of self and I can walk in a new freedom.

THERE IS PLACE

There is a place
Where I can be weak,
Where I will be heard,
Where I can share my heart.

You're not here to fix me.
I don't have to pretend.
It's safe to experience what I feel
And touch the pain.

I can risk revealing
What I have protected the most,
And you treat what I say
And who I am
With respect.

I don't have to defend
What I feel.
You listen and you care
About me.

And I start to believe
I have value,
That I am seen,
That I am understood.

Warmth works into
My frozen pain.
A trickle of hope
Starts to flow,

And my heart longs
For more life
And the healing love
That you and this place offers.

WHY WOULD I EVER GO?
(Repairing Attachment Wounds)

Why would I ever go?
It's safe here.
I love it!

Surrounded by you,
Enfolded in you,
Part of you.

All that is me
Is you too.

You're bigger.
You're stronger.
I'm safe in you.

You know all about me,
You hold my thoughts and feelings.
You love who I am
And I am safe.

I exist because you exist.
Because you know me,
I am safe,
I am alive.

I am wanted.
Because I am part of you,
I can relax.
It's not up to me to survive.

I am content
Because I don't have to know
How to keep myself alive.

You are bigger.
You are stronger.
I must stay.

Because it's here I exist,
It's here I am safe.
It's here I am content.

I never want to go.

SWIMMING IN YOUR GOODNESS

Swimming in your goodness, Lord,
Immersed in your love,

It feels so satisfying,
So right, so good.

Drawing from your wells
Of delight,
At your right hand, Oh Lord,
Are pleasures evermore.

Some are worried
That I'm having too much fun,
That I only think of me
And what I need.

But I drink in
The lavish love, Oh Lord,
That you pour out upon me,
And grow strong
And confident
And filled with joy.

And from a fully satisfied heart
Spilling over with
Contentment and love,

I flow into others' lives
And water their needs
And stir their hunger
For more of what I have.

I point them to the Source...
To my Extravagant Provider
Where there is always enough
To meet your needs and mine
Beyond our wildest imagination.

Swimming in your goodness, Lord,
Immersed in your love.

FEELING SPECIAL

Feeling SPECIAL
Feels SO good!

Trying it on,
Twirling around,
Feet off the ground.

So pleased with myself.
So pleased with you.
So pleased to feel
So special.

Time, attention,
Gentle, available,
Interested, smiling,
Looking, listening,

Hearing, understanding,
Accepting, unhurried,
Staying, caring,

Encouraging me to stay
And be.
Giving the time back
To me.

Feeling SPECIAL
Feels SO good.

Twirling around
Feet off the ground.

Feeling so pleased
To be SO SPECIAL!

AUTHOR'S COMMENTS

As we seek emotional recovery, we are drawn to the life-giving pull of a safe place where we feel wanted, recognized, and important. This dynamic can happen in a counselor's office where early attachment wounds begin to be healed. Our innermost being experiences the relief of not having to figure out life on our own. We can immerse ourselves into another, knowing we will not be taken advantage of and our earliest needs will be met.

Experiencing acceptance without obligation can be a heady experience, like falling in love. Once our deep pain is lanced and we lay down our defenses and receive genuine love and care, we realize how much we have lost.

It may seem foolish for an adult to re-enact and experience for the first time what the Lord intended for us to receive as an infant from a nurturing parent. However, it is part of the process of emotional healing so that we may continue to mature. There is nothing as fulfilling as feeling loved and special.

These intense feelings we experience that are awakened by another person can be transferred to the Lord. Ultimately, the Lord Himself is our safest attachment. He is always loving and available and never fails. He will never abandon us and is always concerned about our well-being.

THOUGHTS TO JOURNAL

• Do I have attachment wounds?

• Have I been taken advantage of emotionally in seeking love and acceptance?

• Is there a safe place, a safe person, who will help me heal without confusing my emotional needs and adult identity?

• Have I been a predator to a wounded person in seeking my own healing?

PRAYER

Dear Lord, don't let me feel ashamed for experiencing strong emotional needs that are released as I being to heal. Help me know the difference between my emotional healing and a healthy loving adult relationship. Forgive me if I have taken emotional advantage of anyone, and heal me if I have been the victim. Let me experience the safety of healing in you, Lord, and the safe people to whom you direct me.

I WANT TO QUIT

I want to quit!
Life is too hard!
I can't keep going,
I didn't expect it to be this way!

You, Lord, called me
To be healed.
I thought it a good idea.
I was doing the right thing.

I was obedient.
It took a lot of courage.
I stepped out in faith
And let you lance the pain.
And now I'm here.
I'm hurt, angry, confused,
And it doesn't feel like you.

Where is your favor?
Where is your grace?
Where are those to support me
In this place?

So much of me longs
To stay in the denial of the past.
But then I feel the greater pain
of missing the mark,

Of disappointing you
And the destiny you've called me to.

Lord, you know my heart.
I want to honor you.
Are you strengthening me, preparing me
Even when I don't see?

I know you love me and are for me.
Hold me, protect me, direct me.

I fix my eyes on you.
I will finish the race
And gladden your heart.
This recovery is hard now,
But you're weaving your art.

One day it will all be
uncovered, processed, and healed,
But until then, dear Lord,
Bring me courage and peace.
Let me rest in you
And my striving cease.

WHO CARES?

Who cares
That I am sad,
That I am lonely,
Misunderstood?

Who has time
To listen to my
Faltering voice
Of need?

They're too busy
To notice
That I am quiet
In the roar of life
Around them.

And if I scream
"I'm sad."
They're angry I
Remind them
I have needs.

"What do you know about
sad?"
"I'll give you something to be
sad about!"

And in my pain
Of shame
I slink away,
Inside
To a dark and lonely place
That feels safe

Where I can pretend
It doesn't matter
That nobody cares.

I CARE

"I hear your cry,
I see your heart."
The Lord tenderly whispers to
My little broken part.

"I hear the
Muffled cries
That you are hiding
Even from your own heart.

"You disappear to a place
Of 'safety.'
You hide there
When no one cares.

"But in hiding
You get lost
And no one even notices.

"Can you believe I care?
Can you trust that
I will hear
Your pain?

"I extend to you a
Listening ear,
A gentle smile,
A kind look,
And all the time you need

"To tell your story,
Feel your story,
Break the silence,
Tell the secrets,
Unlock the truth,
Come out of hiding,
To be loved.

"Because I care!"

YOU WON'T LET ME GO

Lord Jesus,
You won't let me disappear.
You won't let me go.

When all around me
Is terror
And confusion,
You know what to do.

When I am slipping,
Helpless,
Into darkness

Your strong hands
Of love
Reach out to
Save.

You won't let me
Go away.
You won't let me
Go from you.

You hold on
To me.
You connect me
To life.

You infuse safety,
Warmth
And love
Into my heart.

You rescue me
From my own undoing.
You hold on to me.
You won't let me go – EVER.

AUTHOR'S COMMENTS

It takes courage to begin the healing process. We come to realize life is not working for us in our thoughts and behaviors and relationships. Healing recovery sounds like a good thing so we open long-hidden, concealed and barred doors of our emotional past. We can be shocked to discover the impact of revisiting the wounding fields and land mines of the past. It is easy to want to quit the whole recovery process.

Call out to the Lord to keep you steady as you do the hard work of remembering, re-telling, feeling and forgiving. Tell your story in a safe place to a safe person of what happened to you and who has wounded you. Realize it's okay to feel your pain for it is the very avenue of relief and healing.

In recovery, we discover what we believe about ourselves, usually formed in childhood, believing we are not wanted, valued or good enough. We come to these conclusions because of events that happen to us. If we never process our pain with a caring, understanding adult, we base our beliefs on our limited childish wisdom. These childhood beliefs are rarely examined as we grow.

The Lord is with us in our healing journey. He will bring truth and understanding to our immature conclusions and the lies we have believed about ourselves. If we have dissociated because the trauma is too great to bear, the Lord will find us and hold on to us as he brings us to a place of safety and healing.

THOUGHTS TO JOURNAL

• Am I willing to do the hard, but healing, work of recovery?

• What do I believe about myself? Do I know why I believe it? Is it really true?

• What am I still saying about my life that I've been saying since childhood? Has anything changed?

• Do I feel there are parts of me so wounded and lost I will never be healed?

• Do I believe Jesus seeks and saves the lost parts of all who cry out to him?

PRAYER

Dear Lord Jesus, I know your desire for me is to be healed and made whole. You are able to turn what the enemy has intended for evil to my good. Please let me experience how you feel about me, and know the real truth about who I am. Would you find the deepest areas of my unhealed pain, areas of which I may not even be conscious, and bring me to healing? I know you care, and I put my trust in you.

NO SHAME - NO GAME
(To a verbal abuser)

I've had enough!

Who gives you the right
To lord it over me
With your sneering attitude
And caustic words?

What makes you think
You can reduce me to a
Mass of oozing shame
Just because you
Probably feel the same
About yourself?

I'm not your flailing block
That you can pulverize with
Whipping words of pain
Designed to extinguish
The beauty of my being.

Enough of shame!
No more game!
Your power
Over me is broken!

I'm stronger now.
I know the truth.
I am loved and I am lovable.
My worth does not rest in
Your judgment of me.
My value is not determined
By your abuse.

My Father God has adorned me with love
And given me life anew in Christ, my Lord.
He alone is my Lord, He celebrates my being.

He protects me from pain
And strengthens me to
Stand against injustice.

No more shame!
No more game!

PLEASE FORGIVE ME
(From a verbal abuser)

Life and death
Are in the power of the tongue.
Tender hearts have been brutalized
By words of death.

Lord, you never meant it
To be so.
Move on the offender's heart
To say what every wounded soul
Longs to hear.

Let the offender speak what is in your heart,
Lord,
What should be said to each
Wounded victim
As they hear the words of repentance:

"Please forgive me," my abuser says, "for my
sharp tongue
And cutting words,
Causing your heart to bleed
With my insensitivity.

"Please forgive me for intimidating
And bullying you,

Demanding your compliance
Out of my own insecurity.

"Forgive me for mocking, shaming,
Disrespecting, hating you,
Cursing and screaming at you
All the ugly words
That came from my ugly heart.

"It should not have been so.
I have sinned and soiled
Your precious Godly self.

"Please forgive me
For trampling your tender heart,
Ignoring your inner beauty,
Trashing your intrinsic worth,
You, the very gift of God, given to me.

"I have been so careless.
I have been so foolish.
I have been so wrong.

"Can you please forgive me?"

NEVER ENOUGH

Never Enough! Never Enough!
Never Enough!

Time, Attention, Love.

I am needy,
I am desperate
For time with you,
Attention from you,
Love, kindness, care.

There is such an ache
Beneath the sadness
In this place where I don't want to be.

If I don't run away
I'll never survive the pain.
It's so intense I have to
Hide it from myself.

It's so intense
I would be distraught
With my neediness
(And that's not good).

It's so intense I have to
Hide it from others
For they would be consumed
With my neediness
(And that's not nice).

And even if they knew
The extent of the vast, swirling vortex
Of despair,
They could never satisfy it.

I would consume them
And they would be gone
And still it won't be enough...

For
It's never enough!

I AM ENOUGH

"I hear your soul cry, precious one,"
Says Jesus.
"Come to me,
I AM Enough!
I AM not consumable!

"I AM for you,
And I love you.

"Spend time with me.
You are my beloved.

"Come away with me
To our very own place,
Just you and me
Together,
Always.

"Always wanted
Always safe
Always enjoyed
Always time
Always you
Always me.

"For I AM Enough
For you.

"Vast as it is,
I can fill that place of pain
With my love,
My presence,
My touch.

"For I AM always
Enough!"

I CAN'T EAT PROMISES

It's not enough anymore
    To eat promises
And consume expectations,

Patiently waiting for
    The real thing
That will truly satisfy.

Hunger being held at bay
With the hope of "some day"
    No longer works.

Just knowing food is coming
No longer sustains my heart.

It's no longer enough
That someday it will be different,
That someone will probably notice,
That when there's time I will receive,
    That soon it will be my turn.

"Just wait a little longer," they say
    "As soon as I finish
Taking care of everything else, then..."

But I can no longer accommodate
The hope of food,
The wait.
I'm hungry now!
I want to live!

I need you to hear me.
I need you to see I exist,
That my needs are important today,
That I'm here now - not later!

If I cannot eat real food,
I go away to my fantasy banquet
And no one knows I'm hungry.

But now I'm aware of my hungry.
It's no longer enough to pretend.
It doesn't satisfy.

And I'm telling you my secret.
I can't live anymore
On expectations and promises.

HELPLESS WITHOUT SHAME

Getting used to feeling
Helpless
Without shame!

The truth is
I don't know how to
Fix the computer error.

I can't figure it out.
I am stuck
Powerless
Helpless!

Frustrated, annoyed
But not ashamed!

I'm not stupid.
I shouldn't know what to do
To fix what
I never learned.

I can ask for help.
It's okay
To not know.

I'm still all right.
I'm not less than...
Nor vulnerable...
Endangered
For lack of knowledge.

I'm not ashamed for not knowing.
I can be helpless
And still be
All right.

I will learn what I need to know
For each new challenge.
Yet I will need help again
In other areas.

But I am learning
There is no shame
For not knowing
What I never knew.

AUTHOR'S COMMENTS

As children, our sense of self is so dependent upon the adults who are raising us. If we are continually belittled, verbally abused, made to feel stupid for not being more mature than we are able to be, we will begin to believe we are stupid and will never measure up.

It is so healing to have an abuser in our life ask forgiveness. It is even more healing to give that forgiveness.

The Lord strengthens us as we heal, to finally stand up to abuse, to be assertive in healthy ways, and not to shame ourselves believing the abuse is our fault. We stop shaming ourselves for thinking we are supposed to know everything. We can find our voice and express our needs. It's alright to ask for help.

As we matures, if a friend, teacher, pastor, counselor, shows kindness and affirmation, we will be drawn toward that person with deep longings, but also great fear. If we dare to believe we may be acceptable, we can have intense desire to be with that person, unrealistically longing for them to fulfill our needs. Hopefully that person is healthy enough to have clear boundaries and not allow him or herself to be consumed.

In our healing journey, we come to realize our deepest needs are met in the Lord, not people.

THOUGHTS TO JOURNAL

• Have I had abuse in my childhood?

• Am I willing to forgive the offender, even if he or she never asks?

• Am I afraid to speak up for myself, what I need, what I'm feeling? If so, do I know why?

• Do I chase after relationships for my needs to be met?

• Am I willing to offer my heart to the Lord and be dependent on Him?

PRAYER

Dear Lord Jesus, I give you my wounded heart and ask you to forgive me and save me from my sins. I invite you into my heart and ask you to be my Lord and Savior. Heal me from all the abuses of the past. I choose to forgive each person (by name) and for what they have done to damaged me. (name the offenses). Please cleanse me and fill my emptiness and loneness with your love and peace. I acknowledge that you are sufficient for meeting my every need as you lead me in the journey of healing.

DEPENDENT

Can I risk being dependent
On you?
Are you really a safe person?
Is this a safe place?

It is so frightening
To allow myself to need someone,
To let myself be vulnerable,
To actually depend on you to be here for me.

I want to be with you,
Laugh and talk together,
Feel your approval,
See your smile,
Know I'm wanted and accepted.

But I have such fear.
I'm too big to feel so needy.
Yet part of me
Is like an unweaned child,
Needing your presence,
Your comfort, love and care.

When I'm separate, apart,
I don't feel safe, solid, alive,
And I long to hear your voice,
Be in your presence.

If you know the extent
Of how dependent I feel on you,
I fear you will walk away,
Stop being interested in me,
Disappear, stop caring.

And I will be left alone
In excruciating pain,
Filled with shame
That I trusted enough to be
Dependent.

IF I COULD STAY

If I could just stay...
  A little longer,
  Hang around,
  Just be here
  With you,

Then I'd be all right,
  At peace,
  Content,
  Safe.

I don't require much...
  Not a lot of attention,
  But some.
  Any crumb will do.

Once in awhile
  As you pass by,
A look in my direction,
  A smile,
  Would be nice.

I would be okay
If I could stay.
Just knowing you are near,
If I could be here
With you,

I'd be okay.

IT HAS TO BE YOU

It's not the same
If it's not you.

I can't tell just anyone
How I feel.

No one would understand
How important you are to
My existence.

Without you I am broken,
Lost and scared.

When I can't find you,
See you,
Touch you,
Hear you,
I can't find me.

Inside I'm dead,
Sinking, disappearing.

Who else would understand?
This is serious,
I'm not kidding
That I'm not living.

It's not the same
If it's not you.
Substitutes just will not do.

You're the one I've entrusted
With my feelings.
I've given you the power
To keep me from being lost
So I can live.

No one else will do.
It has to be you.

DO I EXIST?

Do I exist?
Do you know who I am?
I've tried to tell you about me
So you can see if I exist.

But when you go
Will you still know
There's a me?

I need you to remember me.

If you still know me
When you're away from me,
Then I can relax
Because I won't
Disappear.

If you still know me
Even when you don't see me
I can exist,
Knowing I'm not forgotten.

If you still know me
Then all my energy
Does not have to be
In surviving,
Alone, forgotten,
Wondering if I'm alive.

If I am found, remembered,
Even when I don't see you,
I can live.
Even when you're away,
I can exist.

And people who exist
Are free
To receive love,
To relax, to laugh,
To expect kindness and goodness
And allow it into
My secret place of hiding.

Because you know me,
You remember me,
I can exist.

LEARNING TO BE NEEDY

I'm usually strong,
I carry on
And never stop to feel
My hurts, pains, inadequacies.

But right now
I feel too weak
To try to make you
Want me.

It requires too much time,
Too much energy,
To think of ways
To get your attention,

And even if I got it,
Can I believe it's because
You really want to give it to me?

I'm tired of trying to obligate you to me
By my caring, fun and winning ways.

So for now
I'm learning to be needy.
I can't keep being the Hero,
Doing everything right,
Carrying all the responsibility.

Perhaps you will want
To understand me
When I don't even understand myself,
To be interested in me,
Even if I'm not performing
on your behalf.

Can I let you know I'm needy,
Tired, and weak?

Are you willing
To be available to me,
Show me kindness,
And allow me to be real too?

I really need that.

HEALTHY DEPENDENCY

"It's okay," says the Lord,
"For you to pour out
Your passion, your love,
Your adoration

"Upon the one who nurtures you,
The one who is there for you,
The one who is safe.

"This is an important part
Of your early development.

"I am letting you experience now
What you once missed.

"I am re-creating for you the joy,
The bliss of dependency,
Of weakness,
Of helplessness,
Without shame or sorrow.

"It's a wonderful state of being
Where ideally all your needs are met
With graciousness and love,

And you take in every goodness
With no fear of it going away.

"You are weak,
You are small,
You are helpless,
And you are safe!

"In Me also, you can experience
And develop healthy dependency.

"For I, the Nurturing One, watch over you
And tenderly care.
There is no stress, anxiety, or fear
For you are dependent
On One who does not fail.

"There is no shame in all your needs,
All your thoughts,
All your ways,
For you are loved without condition.
You are enjoyed without judgment.
You are freed to love and grow
And remember…

"The joy, the bliss of healthy dependency
On Me, your Nurturing God.

JUST HANGING OUT

Just hanging out.
No sparkle,
No entertaining,
No discussion of interest.

Just quieting down,
Unhurried,
Being close,
Feeling open,
Being wanted.

Enjoyed for doing nothing.
Enjoyed for hanging out
And being me.

No agenda, no plans
Nothing to get done.
Just me,
Just you,
And time
Unhurried,
To unfold and be
Just me.

Sometimes terrific,
Sometimes dull,
Maybe even wonderful
At times.

But no need to get all excited
About it
Either way.

Just hanging out.
Just me,
Just you,
And time unhurried.

NO MORE GAMES

No more games.
Here I am
Just as I am,
Sometimes feeling
Small, weak, vulnerable,
At your mercy,
No defense.

I'm letting you look and see
That inside part of me
Often so well hidden
From others
And even myself.

If I make a fool of myself,
So be it.
I don't want to,
But I'm not perfect,
And sometimes I fail...
You and myself too.

Go ahead and see
The good and the bad...
The real me,

Ordinary human
Who feels deeply, desires love,
And is tired of hiding.

If you can see
All sides of me
And STILL
Want to know me,
Be with me,

THEN I can believe
I am perhaps
Lovable,
Worth value,
Wanted by someone,
Wanted by you.

More . . .

Let me test your acceptance
Of me
By my honesty.
I will never know the truth
If I keep pretending
And only let you
See the parts
I think you will want,
Accept, love.

No more games.
Here I am.
Take me or leave me.

I hope you will choose
To like me.
I am risking revealing
Me.

But it is a good risk,
Moving into life...
Life lived in honesty,
Freedom, truth, acceptance,
Walking in the light
With myself,
You,
And the Lord.

REFLECTION

(this is a space for you to write your thoughts)

AUTHOR'S COMMENTS

It seems strange, a paradox, that in our deep neediness for relationships, we pride ourselves on our independence, believing we need no one. Healing begins when we learn we can allow ourselves to be needy with a safe person, one who will not take advantage of us. (This healing can be experienced in a safe and caring counselor's office.) As adults, we can revisit what we did not receive in childhood. The needs of our inner infant experiences safety and identity by dependence on another person who understands the dynamics of transference. (Transference is transferring onto another person the role of being who we need them to be. This can be positive or negative.)

If there is not healthy attachment to a caring, nurturing person in our infancy and childhood we will not develop the trust needed for healthy relationships. However, if a person shows us attention and care, we begin to find our identity in their attentive presence. As we are loved, we discover we are a separate person who has value and worth. We are at peace within ourselves, not needing to measure up to another's standard.

THOUGHTS TO JOURNAL

• Have I ever found myself trying to "absorb" myself into someone else's life?

• Am I experiencing true love, or is it an attachment disorder?

• Do I consider myself "fiercely independent?" If so, do I know why?

• Do I feel ashamed to have to sometimes rely on another person?

• Do I feel comfortable in my own skin?

PRAYER

Dear Father God, draw me to find all my attachment needs in you. It is safe to pour out my neediness to you. You will never take advantage of me. Allow me to be dependent on you and experience your strength and love. Bring me into healthy interdependency in my relationships, and heal me to be at peace with myself, the person you created me to be.

I SLIPPED AWAY

I slipped away
So quickly,
So quietly.

Part by part of me
Left
And went away.

I couldn't be brave enough,
So my terrified part
Disappeared.
I was supposed to be happy, compliant,
So my pain and grief
Hide away.

Piece by piece
The parts of me
That couldn't exist
In conscious awareness
Quietly broke off
And disappeared.

Where did I go?
I don't know.
But it was dark and sad
And lonely.

I waited for them to notice
Part of me had gone.
I waited for them to want
The whole of me.

Surely they would
Search for me.
Surely they must
Miss me.

But they seemed to only want
The part of me who stayed
And played
The game they wanted.

But parts of me
Had quietly
Slipped away
And they didn't know
I was gone.

I MUST FORGET YOU

Now that parts of me
Are gone,
I must forget you were ever here.

No one seemed to know
I had split off.
Now even I don't know.

If I allowed myself to remember you
I wouldn't be able to handle the terror,
Betrayal
Sadness and pain
That you hold.

You're too much for me to bear.
I'm glad you went away.
Please stay
Beyond my memory
Of why you left.

Leave me alone.
Don't let me feel what you hold.
I can't handle your intensity.
You're too much for me.

I would not survive
If I knew the truth you hold.
I have no skills
To endure the pain.

I needed supportive adults,
But they never came
To help me process
Why you left.

Because you're gone
I don't have to
Feel or hurt.

That's why I must
Forget you.

I HEARD YOU CRYING

I heard you crying
The other day.
I thought I had disconnected and
Forgotten you.

I felt you burning
In my heart
And I was shocked
To know you still
Existed.

What do you want
From me?
You left,
And it seemed
For the best.

I've gone on with life
Without you.
Why are you calling
My name?

How can I let myself
know again
The pain you hold?

I'm ashamed of you.
I've denied you ever existed.

Yet I hear you crying,
And you start to burn
In my heart.
I hesitate with compassion,
And draw back in terror.

Is it true you still exist,
Can you tell me why you left?
Do you want to be part
of my life now?
Is it possible
We could be one
Again?

IF I EMBRACE THE PAIN

O God in Heaven,
Help me!

I've heard my soul cry
And I cannot turn away.

What do I do now?
It is more than I can bear
To enter again
Into the pain I left there
So long ago.

All that I know wants to run
Like I've done all my life
From the wounded, separated parts
Of me
Who plead to exist.

It feels like I will die
If I embrace the pain.
I've worked so hard
To live without it.

Please, God, give me grace and strength
To enter
Into myself again
And grieve what I've been afraid
To remember, touch and feel.

I must lay my life down, Lord,
For the parts that will die
Without me.

Please give us life.
Knit the raveled broken parts of me
Together
That I might live as whole,
That I might be complete in myself,
That I might be complete in you!

ONCE YOU WERE LOST

Once you were lost
But now you are found.
God hears your cry.

The Good Shepherd knew
You had gone away.

You were never beyond
His seeking heart.

He saw you break apart
And leave.
He gathered your little ones
One by one
Into a safe place
And watched over you.

He stayed with you in your pain.
He knew where you were,
Waiting for the day
He could bring you again
To yourself.

He moved in your life,
Circumstance by circumstance,
Prayer by prayer,
Day by day,

Until you were able to hear
Your soul cry
Even as he had heard it
From the beginning.

And Jesus dawned upon you
That joyous day
When your lost parts were found
And you were reunited
With love and life and you.

EXTRAVAGANT LOVER

Lord, free me to be
An Extravagant Lover,

To pour out the passion
Which you have poured within,

To lavish you with exaltations
Of the Highest Praise,

To adore you with tender love
And honor you with words of delight.

You have created me
To worship.
You have created me
To love.
You have given me the
Emotions, heart and desire
To honor you with praise.

I was designed to experience
at my mother's breast,
The joy of being wanted,
Drinking in the tender love
And nourishment you created me to receive.

I clung to her for life
And received my deepest needs.
I found safety and acceptance
In her arms,
To be wanted, loved, cherished.

You built in me the capacity
To love and adore
In response to tender nurture.

I have spent a lifetime seeking
That love again,
Or maybe for the first time.

More . . .

Open my eyes to see
that love is in you!
The One who created me to respond.
The only One in whom I will be
Fully satisfied.

Free me to be
An Extravagant Lover.

As you pour in your nurturing Life,
Let me pour it out in gratitude
To you,
And in love to others.

Free me to be an
Extravagant Lover,

To you,
My Extravagant God!

REFLECTION

(this is a space for you to write your thoughts)

AUTHOR'S COMMENTS

There is a term called dissociation. Dissociation can happen in our early childhood when we experience an intolerable conflict, a trauma so great that the memory and feeling of the event splits off into a part of the brain that is not connected to the conscious mind.

Dissociation is a God-given defense mechanism that helps us maintain a sense of normalcy. When we experience a dysfunctional, cruel, abusive, dangerous, or evil situation as a child, the trauma memory will quickly dissociate so we can go on with life. The dissociation is intended to be a short-term safety valve until we are old enough, strong enough, safe enough, and have a safe person with whom we can process the events.

Uncomfortable or frightening events in our adult life can often trigger a lost memory into conscious recall. Other times, we may have disturbing dreams. If we are willing to pursue the roots of our current distress, the lost memory may surface in a visual or emotional way. It can be very painful to become aware of the terrifying event or events. Yet there can be some relief by helping us realize why we act and behave the way we do in the present. When the memories remain hidden, dissociated, they still impact us subconsciously in many ways and we don't know why we have trouble living life.

The good news is that our Lord desires for us to be whole in body, soul, and spirit. He desires for us to know the truth of our past. Jesus is with us as we allow our dissociated memories to come into consciousness. We can seek knowledgeable help to process the terror, grieve the loss and pain, and ultimately release our offenders in forgiveness.

THOUGHTS TO JOURNAL

• How much of my childhood do I remember? If it is limited, ask the Lord to bring the lost or dissociated memories to consciousness.

• Do I fear discovery of what may have happened to me? Am I willing to know the truth?

• What feelings am I having when I consider exploring my early life?

PRAYER

Dear Jesus, I desire to have truth in my inmost being so that I may be truly healed. I invite you to come with me into this journey of the past, to the roots of my pain. I trust you to protect me as I remember. Be my comfort. Find all the lost parts of me and bring me to safety. Cleanse me and hold me as I grieve my losses. Help me understand it was not my fault. As I process the abuse, help me release in forgiveness all who harmed me, intentionally or unintentionally, so I will no longer be oppressed by their behavior. Thank you Lord for your unfailing love to me. Thank you that you have heard my soul cry out to you and you are with me to heal and bring full restoration.

ONE DAY YOUR SOUL WILL SING

"Oh, My little child,
I see your tears
I know your fears.
I hear your soul cry.

"I am a God of Mercy.
I knew your "secrets" before you had them,
And I never stopped loving you.

"I wept with you in your pain.
I gave help in your struggles.
I made a Way through temptation and sin
So you could find your way back to Me.

"Who told you that I commanded you to never fail?
I created you to be dependent and real
So that you would love Me
And discover life
Is experienced best
In relationship with Me.

"I knew your wounds
And planned ahead regarding your failures.
Even now I bring healing to your broken heart.
I restore, redeem, and make new.

"There is mercy and comfort in me
And from the many wounded healers
Who have received my healing, mercy and grace.

"Allow me and them
To hear your soul cry,
As long as you need to cry,
Until one day –
A beautiful and amazing thing,

"With hope and joy
And happy tears,
Your soul begins to sing."

CHOICE AND CHOSEN

"You are a choice and chosen vessel
Fully and adequately prepared
To do all that I've called you to do,"
Says the Lord.

"You serve from a healed heart
That once was wounded and broken.
You hear the cries of my people.
You are tender toward their pain.

You, like I, have been touched by the
Feelings of their infirmity.
You weep with those who weep.
You rejoice with those who rejoice.
I am conforming you into my image
That you will know victory through sorrow and pain.

And to the pain of others
You will extend my hand of mercy and grace,
Even as I have extended it to you,
My precious child.

Know that you are a choice and chosen vessel,
Fully and adequately equipped
To do my will.

I love you
And I'm so proud of you.
I will always be with you,
Forever!"

About The Author

Trudy Colflesh has had a tender heart and sensitive spirit since childhood. She grew up in the home of a Presbyterian minister and saw her parents seek to meet others' needs in Christian love and service.

Trudy became active in service herself in high school and college. She graduated from the College of Wooster, Ohio, married her college sweetheart and worked several years in a Presbyterian church as a Director of Christian Education.

For many years, Trudy was a stay-at-home mom and active in volunteer church service. She and her husband, George, have two natural children, Christopher and Karen, a son Michael, adopted when he was ten years old, and have fostered two young boys.

When Karen was almost seven, she became ill with leukemia and despite doing all possible to save her, she died within seven months. Out of this painful time, Trudy wrote the book *Too Precious To Die* and traveled around the country speaking at Women's Aglow Fellowships and appearing on CBN and other TV and radio programs.

Having opportunity to minister to hurting people, as she herself was healing, Trudy felt the Lord calling her to go into the field of counseling. She went to graduate school and earned her Master's degree in Counseling at Montclair State University, New Jersey, in 1990 and became a Licensed Professional Counselor.

Since that time, Trudy has worked as a Christian Counselor, ministering hope and healing to countless clients. She has listened to her own soul cry and pursued recovery, as well as listened to the hearts of her clients. She knows with certainty, that out of the painful issues of life, comes a sure belief that Jesus Christ knows our emotional pain, hears our soul cry and brings us His Presence to comfort and heal.

"And we know that in all things God works for the good of those who love him, who have been called according to his purpose." (Romans 8:28)

Trudy is available for telephone counseling and coaching. If you would like to set up an appointment, please contact her at Trudy@Encouraginghope.com. Comments or questions may also be addressed to Trudy at this location.

SEE OTHER BOOKS IN THE SoulCry Series

Book 1
Shame, Confusion, Numbness, Escape, Anger, Loneliness, Lostness

Book 2
Abandonment, Broken Relationships, Fear, Rejection, Emotional Wounding, Soul Splitting, Forgiveness, Comfort, Love

Book 4
Sexual Abuse, Denial, Ritual Abuse, Dissociation, Betrayal, Control, Identity, Trauma

Book 5
Sexual Abuse, Ritual Abuse, Dissociation, Suffering, Forgiveness, Comfort, Healing, Joy

Book 6
Shame, Failure, Perfection, Ritual Abuse, Anger, Dissociation, Sexual Intimacy, Truth, Acceptance

Book 7
Worth, Denial, Dissociation, Ritual Abuse, Rejection, Sexual Abuse, Surrender, Love, Healing

Book 8

Enmeshment, Attachment, Self Worth, Suffering, Occult Bondage, Generational Iniquities, Mercy, Freedom, Integration

Book 9

Denial, Guilt, Shame, Lost Identity, Lost Time, Reputation, Dissociation, Programming, Comfort, Safety, Original Self

All books are available to order at:

WWW.ENCOURAGINGHOPE.COM/SOULCRY

ALSO AVAILABLE BY TRUDY COLFLESH

Too Precious To Die

Seven year old Karen Colflesh was diagnosed with AML, Acute Myelomonocytic Leukemia, a rare form of the disease not usually found in children.

Too Precious To Die, is an intimate, personal account of Karen's battle against this deadly disease. It is as triumphant as it is tragic.

Karen's courageous fight was an inspiration to all who came in contact with her.

This story shows the victories the Lord God won on Karen's behalf, and the healing miracles He demonstrated throughout her illness.

However, despite all the doctor's skill and the faith of many, Karen was called home to Heaven in a glorious vision.

Trudy shares how she and the family overcame their grief and found answers and comfort to Karen's early death.

Trudy has shared Karen's story throughout the country, speaking at Women's Aglow meetings, as well as on radio and TV.

She and her husband George were guests of Pat Robinson on the 700 Club.

This is a moving, compelling story that draws the reader into the experience. *(paperback, 248 pages)*